Chapter 1: Introduction to Retiring in Portugal

Why Choose Portugal for Retirement

If you are considering retiring abroad, Portugal should definitely be at the top of your list. This beautiful country offers a high quality of life, stunning landscapes, and a welcoming culture that make it an ideal destination for retirees. But why choose Portugal for retirement? Let's explore some of the reasons that make this country a perfect choice for those looking for a new beginning in their golden years.

First and foremost, Portugal is known for its affordable cost of living. From housing to healthcare to dining out, you will find that your retirement savings can stretch much further in Portugal than in many other European countries. This means that you can enjoy a comfortable lifestyle without breaking the bank, allowing you to truly relax and enjoy your retirement years to the fullest.

Retiring Abroad: Portugal Edition for Adults Looking for a New Beginning

Another reason to choose Portugal for retirement is the country's excellent healthcare system. Portugal boasts high-quality medical care, with modern facilities and highly trained professionals. As a retiree in Portugal, you can rest assured that you will have access to top-notch healthcare services whenever you need them, giving you peace of mind and ensuring that you can enjoy your retirement without worrying about medical issues.

In addition to its affordability and excellent healthcare system, Portugal also offers a rich cultural experience for retirees. From historic cities like Lisbon and Porto to charming villages in the countryside, Portugal is full of opportunities to immerse yourself in the country's unique culture and history. Whether you enjoy exploring museums and art galleries or sampling local cuisine and wines, Portugal has something for everyone.

Retiring Abroad: Portugal Edition for Adults Looking for a New Beginning

Lastly, Portugal's mild climate and stunning natural beauty make it a paradise for outdoor enthusiasts. Whether you enjoy hiking in the mountains, relaxing on the beach, or simply taking a leisurely stroll through a picturesque village, Portugal's diverse landscapes offer endless opportunities for outdoor recreation. With over 300 days of sunshine per year, you can enjoy the great outdoors all year round, making Portugal the perfect destination for active retirees.

In conclusion, Portugal offers a perfect combination of affordability, healthcare, culture, and outdoor recreation that make it an ideal choice for retirees looking for a new beginning. Whether you are drawn to the country's stunning landscapes, rich history, or warm climate, Portugal has something to offer everyone. So why choose Portugal for retirement? The real question is, why wouldn't you? Start planning your retirement in Portugal today and embark on the adventure of a lifetime.

Benefits of Retiring in Portugal

Retiring Abroad: Portugal Edition for Adults Looking for a New Beginning

Are you considering retiring abroad and looking for a new beginning? Portugal may just be the perfect destination for you. There are numerous benefits to retiring in Portugal that make it an attractive option for adults seeking a change of scenery and a relaxed lifestyle. In this subchapter, we will explore some of the key advantages of retiring in Portugal that make it a top choice for many expats.

One of the biggest benefits of retiring in Portugal is the affordable cost of living. Compared to other European countries, Portugal offers a lower cost of living while still providing a high quality of life. From housing to healthcare to dining out, you can enjoy a comfortable lifestyle without breaking the bank. This makes Portugal an appealing option for retirees on a budget who still want to enjoy all the amenities of a European lifestyle.

Retiring Abroad: Portugal Edition for Adults Looking for a New Beginning

Another advantage of retiring in Portugal is the country's mild climate. With over 300 days of sunshine a year, Portugal offers a warm and sunny climate that is perfect for outdoor activities and relaxation. Whether you enjoy spending time at the beach, exploring historic towns, or simply soaking up the sun in your backyard, Portugal's climate allows you to enjoy the outdoors year-round.

Portugal also boasts a welcoming and friendly local population, making it easy for expats to integrate into the community and feel at home. From the bustling cities to the quaint rural villages, you'll find that Portuguese people are warm, hospitable, and eager to share their culture with newcomers. This sense of community and belonging can make retiring in Portugal a truly enriching experience.

Retiring Abroad: Portugal Edition for Adults Looking for a New Beginning

Retiring Abroad: Portugal Edition for Adults Looking for a New Beginning

Retiring Abroad: Portugal Edition for Adults Looking for a New Beginning

In addition to its welcoming locals and affordable cost of living, Portugal offers a high standard of healthcare that is easily accessible to retirees. The country's healthcare system is ranked as one of the best in the world, with modern facilities and well-trained medical professionals. Whether you need routine check-ups, specialized treatments, or emergency care, you can rest assured that you will receive top-notch healthcare services in Portugal.

Overall, retiring in Portugal offers a unique opportunity to enjoy a high quality of life at an affordable price, all while basking in the country's warm climate and welcoming community. If you're looking for a new beginning in a beautiful and culturally rich country, Portugal may just be the perfect place for you to retire and start the next chapter of your life.

Challenges of Retiring Abroad

Retiring abroad can be an exciting and rewarding experience, but it also comes with its own set of challenges. For adults looking to start a new chapter of their lives in Portugal, it's important to be aware of some of the obstacles you may encounter along the way.

Retiring Abroad: Portugal Edition for Adults Looking for a New Beginning

One of the biggest challenges of retiring abroad is adjusting to a new culture and way of life. Moving to a foreign country means leaving behind the familiar and embracing the unknown. It can be challenging to navigate a new language, customs, and social norms, but with an open mind and willingness to learn, you can adapt and thrive in your new environment.

Another challenge of retiring abroad is the distance from family and friends. Moving to a new country means leaving behind your support system and the people you care about most. It can be tough to be far away from loved ones, especially during important events or in times of need. However, with modern technology, staying connected has never been easier, and you can always plan visits or encourage loved ones to come and see you in your new home.

Retiring Abroad: Portugal Edition for Adults Looking for a New Beginning

Retiring Abroad: Portugal Edition for Adults Looking for a New Beginning

Retiring Abroad: Portugal Edition for Adults Looking for a New Beginning

Financial considerations are also a significant challenge when retiring abroad. From navigating foreign tax laws to managing currency exchange rates, there are many financial factors to consider when moving to a new country. It's important to create a budget and plan for unexpected expenses to ensure a smooth transition and a comfortable retirement.

Healthcare is another challenge to consider when retiring abroad. Access to quality healthcare services can vary greatly from country to country, so it's important to research healthcare options and insurance coverage before making the move. Finding a doctor you trust and understanding the healthcare system in your new country can help ensure your well-being and peace of mind in retirement.

Retiring Abroad: Portugal Edition for Adults Looking for a New Beginning

In conclusion, retiring abroad in Portugal can be a wonderful opportunity for a new beginning, but it's essential to be aware of the challenges you may face along the way. By being prepared, flexible, and proactive in addressing these obstacles, you can make the most of your retirement years in your new home. Remember, with the right mindset and support system, you can overcome any challenges that come your way and enjoy a fulfilling and enriching retirement experience in Portugal.

Retiring Abroad: Portugal Edition for Adults Looking for a New Beginning

Retiring Abroad: Portugal Edition for Adults Looking for a New Beginning

Chapter 2: Planning Your Move to Portugal

Researching Different Regions in Portugal

Researching different regions in Portugal is an essential step in planning your retirement in this beautiful country. Each region in Portugal offers a unique experience, from the bustling city life of Lisbon to the serene beaches of the Algarve. By taking the time to explore the various regions, you can find the perfect place to call home during your retirement years.

Retiring Abroad: Portugal Edition for Adults Looking for a New Beginning

One of the most popular regions for retirees in Portugal is the Algarve. Known for its stunning beaches, warm climate, and affordable cost of living, the Algarve has long been a favorite destination for expats. Whether you prefer the quaint charm of a coastal village or the amenities of a larger city, the Algarve has something for everyone.

If you're looking for a more urban retirement experience, Lisbon may be the perfect choice for you. As the capital city of Portugal, Lisbon offers a vibrant culture, excellent public transportation, and a thriving expat community. With its historic architecture, delicious cuisine, and lively nightlife, Lisbon is a city that never fails to impress.

For those seeking a quieter, more traditional way of life, the interior regions of Portugal may be the ideal choice. Towns like Coimbra, Evora, and Tomar offer a slower pace of life, surrounded by beautiful countryside and historic landmarks. These regions are perfect for those who want to immerse themselves in Portuguese culture and truly experience the authentic way of life in this country.

Retiring Abroad: Portugal Edition for Adults Looking for a New Beginning

No matter which region you choose to retire in, it's important to do thorough research to ensure that it meets your needs and preferences. By exploring the different regions of Portugal, you can find the perfect place to start your new beginning and enjoy a fulfilling retirement in this captivating country.

Understanding Visa and Residency Requirements

Understanding Visa and Residency Requirements is a crucial step for anyone considering retiring abroad, especially in a country like Portugal. As an adult looking for a new beginning in this beautiful country, it is important to familiarize yourself with the different types of visas and residency options available to you. By understanding these requirements, you can ensure a smooth transition to your new life in Portugal.

Retiring Abroad: Portugal Edition for Adults Looking for a New Beginning

One of the most common visas for retirees in Portugal is the D7 visa, also known as the passive income visa. This visa is ideal for individuals who have a stable source of income, such as a pension or investments, and wish to retire in Portugal. The D7 visa allows you to live in the country for one year, with the possibility of renewal for up to two years at a time. It is important to note that you must be able to prove that you have sufficient funds to support yourself during your stay in Portugal.

Another option for retirees looking to move to Portugal is the Golden Visa program. This program grants residency to individuals who make a significant investment in the country, such as buying real estate or starting a business. The Golden Visa allows you to live and work in Portugal, as well as travel freely throughout the Schengen area. This visa is particularly appealing to those looking to establish a permanent residence in Portugal.

Retiring Abroad: Portugal Edition for Adults Looking for a New Beginning

In addition to visas, it is important to understand the residency requirements for retirees in Portugal. To qualify for residency, you must demonstrate that you have a reliable source of income and access to healthcare. You will also need to register with the local authorities and obtain a residence permit. By fulfilling these requirements, you can enjoy all the benefits of living in Portugal as a legal resident.

Overall, understanding visa and residency requirements is essential for anyone looking to retire in Portugal. By familiarizing yourself with the different options available to you, you can make an informed decision about your future in this beautiful country. Whether you choose to apply for a D7 visa, invest in the Golden Visa program, or pursue another residency option, Portugal offers a welcoming and vibrant community for retirees seeking a new beginning.

Financial Considerations for Retiring in Portugal

Retiring Abroad: Portugal Edition for Adults Looking for a New Beginning

When considering retiring in Portugal, there are several important financial considerations to keep in mind. One of the key factors to take into account is the cost of living in Portugal. While Portugal is known for being more affordable than many other European countries, it is still important to carefully budget and plan for your retirement expenses. This includes taking into account housing costs, healthcare expenses, and everyday living expenses such as groceries and transportation.

Another important financial consideration for retiring in Portugal is understanding the tax implications of living in the country. Portugal offers several tax incentives for retirees, including a special tax regime for non-habitual residents that can greatly reduce your tax burden. It is important to work with a financial advisor or tax professional to fully understand how these tax laws will impact your retirement finances.

Retiring Abroad: Portugal Edition for Adults Looking for a New Beginning

One of the benefits of retiring in Portugal is the access to high-quality healthcare at a fraction of the cost of many other countries. Portugal has a public healthcare system that is available to residents, as well as private healthcare options for those who prefer a higher level of care. It is important to factor in healthcare costs when planning for your retirement in Portugal, including insurance premiums, co-pays, and any out-of-pocket expenses.

When it comes to managing your finances in retirement, it is important to consider the currency exchange rate between your home country and Portugal. Fluctuations in exchange rates can impact the value of your retirement savings and pension income, so it is important to have a plan in place to mitigate this risk. Working with a financial advisor who specializes in international finance can help you navigate these challenges and ensure that your retirement savings are protected.

Retiring Abroad: Portugal Edition for Adults Looking for a New Beginning

In conclusion, retiring in Portugal can be a wonderful opportunity for adults looking for a new beginning. By carefully considering the financial implications of retiring in Portugal, including the cost of living, tax laws, healthcare expenses, and currency exchange rates, you can ensure a smooth transition into your retirement years. With proper planning and the right financial guidance, retiring in Portugal can be a financially secure and fulfilling experience.

Retiring Abroad: Portugal Edition for Adults Looking for a New Beginning

Chapter 3: Finding the Right Accommodation in Portugal

Renting vs. Buying Property in Portugal

Retiring Abroad: Portugal Edition for Adults Looking for a New Beginning

When considering retiring in Portugal, one of the biggest decisions you will have to make is whether to rent or buy property. Both options have their pros and cons, and it ultimately comes down to your personal preferences and financial situation. Renting a property in Portugal can offer flexibility and freedom, as you are not tied down to a specific location or property long-term. This can be appealing for those who are unsure about where they want to settle or who prefer to have the option to move around.

On the other hand, buying property in Portugal can be a great investment for your retirement years. Owning your own home gives you a sense of stability and security, and you have the freedom to customize and renovate the property to your liking. Additionally, property prices in Portugal have been steadily increasing over the years, making it a potentially lucrative investment for the future. However, it's important to consider the costs associated with buying a property, such as maintenance, property taxes, and insurance.

Retiring Abroad: Portugal Edition for Adults Looking for a New Beginning

If you are considering renting in Portugal, it's important to research the rental market and familiarize yourself with the rental laws and regulations in the country. Make sure to budget for monthly rent payments, as well as any additional costs such as utilities, internet, and maintenance. It's also a good idea to work with a real estate agent who specializes in rentals, as they can help you find the perfect property that meets your needs and budget.

On the other hand, if you are leaning towards buying property in Portugal, it's essential to work with a reputable real estate agent who can guide you through the buying process. Consider factors such as location, property size, amenities, and neighborhood when searching for your dream retirement home. Take your time to visit different properties and neighborhoods to get a feel for what suits your lifestyle and preferences. Ultimately, whether you choose to rent or buy property in Portugal, it's important to make a decision that aligns with your financial goals and retirement plans.

Popular Expat Communities in Portugal

Retiring Abroad: Portugal Edition for Adults Looking for a New Beginning

Portugal has become an increasingly popular destination for expats looking to retire in a beautiful and affordable location. The country offers a high quality of life, stunning natural landscapes, delicious cuisine, and a rich cultural heritage. For those considering making the move to Portugal, there are several popular expat communities that offer a welcoming and supportive environment for retirees.

One of the most well-known expat communities in Portugal is the Algarve region, located in the southern part of the country. The Algarve is known for its picturesque beaches, charming villages, and warm climate, making it a popular choice for retirees looking to enjoy a relaxed and laid-back lifestyle. There are several expat communities in the Algarve, such as Vilamoura, Albufeira, and Lagos, where retirees can find like-minded individuals and enjoy a variety of social activities.

Retiring Abroad: Portugal Edition for Adults Looking for a New Beginning

Another popular expat community in Portugal is Lisbon, the country's capital city. Lisbon offers a vibrant cultural scene, excellent healthcare facilities, and a range of entertainment options for retirees. The city is also well-connected to other parts of Portugal and Europe, making it easy for expats to travel and explore the surrounding areas. In Lisbon, retirees can enjoy a mix of traditional Portuguese culture and modern amenities, making it a great choice for those looking for a cosmopolitan lifestyle.

For those seeking a more peaceful and rural setting, the Alentejo region in central Portugal is a popular choice among expat retirees. The Alentejo is known for its rolling hills, vineyards, and historic towns, providing a tranquil and scenic backdrop for those looking to retire in a quiet and idyllic setting. There are several expat communities in the Alentejo, such as Évora, Beja, and Monsaraz, where retirees can enjoy a slower pace of life and connect with nature.

Retiring Abroad: Portugal Edition for Adults Looking for a New Beginning

Overall, Portugal offers a range of expat communities to suit every retiree's preferences and lifestyle. Whether you prefer the beachy vibes of the Algarve, the cosmopolitan atmosphere of Lisbon, or the peaceful countryside of the Alentejo, there is a community in Portugal that will welcome you with open arms. Retiring abroad in Portugal is a wonderful opportunity to start a new chapter in your life, surrounded by stunning scenery, delicious food, and friendly locals.

Tips for Finding a Real Estate Agent in Portugal

If you are considering retiring in Portugal, one of the most important decisions you will make is choosing a real estate agent to help you find the perfect home. Finding a reputable and trustworthy agent can make all the difference in your experience of buying property in a foreign country. Here are some tips to help you find the right real estate agent in Portugal.

Retiring Abroad: Portugal Edition for Adults Looking for a New Beginning

First and foremost, do your research. Take the time to look for real estate agents who specialize in helping expats and retirees find properties in Portugal. You can start by asking for recommendations from friends or family who have already made the move, or by searching online for agents with positive reviews and a good track record.

Once you have a list of potential agents, take the time to interview them. Ask about their experience working with retirees, their knowledge of the local market, and their communication style. It's important to find an agent who understands your needs and preferences and who can communicate effectively with you throughout the buying process.

When choosing a real estate agent in Portugal, it's also important to consider their fees and commission structure. Make sure you understand how much you will be paying for their services and what services are included in their fee. It's also a good idea to clarify any additional costs or fees that may arise during the buying process.

Retiring Abroad: Portugal Edition for Adults Looking for a New Beginning

Finally, trust your instincts. When choosing a real estate agent in Portugal, it's important to feel comfortable and confident in your decision. If you have any doubts or concerns about an agent, don't be afraid to move on and find someone else who better suits your needs. Remember, finding the right real estate agent can make all the difference in your experience of retiring in Portugal.

Chapter 4: Navigating Healthcare in Portugal

Overview of the Portuguese Healthcare System

The Portuguese healthcare system is known for providing high-quality care to its residents and visitors. As a retiree considering moving to Portugal, it is important to understand how the healthcare system works in order to ensure you have access to the medical services you may need. This overview will provide you with a general understanding of how healthcare is structured in Portugal.

Retiring Abroad: Portugal Edition for Adults Looking for a New Beginning

In Portugal, healthcare is provided through a combination of public and private services. The National Health Service (SNS) is the public healthcare system that provides universal coverage to all residents. The SNS is funded through taxes and provides a wide range of medical services, including doctor visits, hospital care, and prescription medications. Additionally, there are private healthcare providers that offer services for those who prefer to pay for faster access to care or additional services.

One of the key benefits of the Portuguese healthcare system is its affordability. The cost of healthcare in Portugal is relatively low compared to other European countries, making it an attractive option for retirees on a fixed income. Additionally, prescription medications are also more affordable in Portugal, which can help lower the overall cost of healthcare for retirees.

Retiring Abroad: Portugal Edition for Adults Looking for a New Beginning

Access to healthcare in Portugal is generally good, with a high number of doctors and hospitals per capita. This means that retirees in Portugal can expect to receive timely and quality care when needed. Additionally, many healthcare professionals in Portugal speak English, making it easier for English-speaking retirees to communicate with their doctors and medical staff.

Overall, the Portuguese healthcare system offers retirees a high standard of care at an affordable price. Whether you choose to use the public healthcare system or opt for private insurance, you can feel confident that you will have access to the medical services you need in Portugal. By familiarizing yourself with how the healthcare system works in Portugal, you can make informed decisions about your healthcare options as a retiree living in this beautiful country.

Finding Health Insurance in Portugal

Retiring Abroad: Portugal Edition for Adults Looking for a New Beginning

Finding health insurance in Portugal is a crucial step for adults looking to retire in this beautiful country. As a retiree, it's important to ensure that you have access to quality healthcare services to maintain your well-being. Fortunately, Portugal offers a robust healthcare system that provides both public and private options for residents.

The public healthcare system in Portugal is known for its high quality and accessibility. As a resident, you are entitled to free or low-cost healthcare services at public hospitals and clinics. To access these services, you will need to register with the Portuguese National Health Service (SNS) and obtain a user card. This card will give you access to a range of medical services, including doctor's appointments, hospital stays, and prescription medications.

Retiring Abroad: Portugal Edition for Adults Looking for a New Beginning

In addition to the public healthcare system, many retirees choose to supplement their coverage with private health insurance in Portugal. Private health insurance offers additional benefits, such as access to a wider network of doctors and hospitals, shorter wait times for appointments, and coverage for services not included in the public system. When choosing a private health insurance plan, it's important to consider factors such as cost, coverage options, and customer service.

To find the right health insurance plan for your needs, it's recommended to consult with a local insurance broker or financial advisor who specializes in healthcare coverage for expats. They can help you navigate the complexities of the Portuguese healthcare system and find a plan that meets your specific needs and budget. Additionally, it's a good idea to research different insurance providers and compare their offerings before making a decision.

In conclusion, finding health insurance in Portugal is an essential part of preparing for retirement in this beautiful country. By exploring both public and private healthcare options, consulting with experts, and conducting thorough research, you can ensure that you have access to quality healthcare services that meet your needs as a retiree. Prioritizing your health and well-being will allow you to fully enjoy your retirement in Portugal and make the most of this new chapter in your life.

Accessing Medical Care as an Expat in Portugal

Accessing medical care as an expat in Portugal is a crucial aspect of retiring abroad. As an adult looking for a new beginning in this beautiful country, it is important to familiarize yourself with the healthcare system to ensure you have the support you need as you settle into your new life. Portugal offers a high standard of healthcare, with both public and private options available to expats.

Retiring Abroad: Portugal Edition for Adults Looking for a New Beginning

One of the key benefits of the Portuguese healthcare system is the accessibility of care. Expats are eligible to access the public healthcare system, which provides quality medical services at a fraction of the cost compared to other countries. Additionally, Portugal has a large network of healthcare facilities, including hospitals, clinics, and pharmacies, making it easy to access medical care no matter where you are located in the country.

For those who prefer private healthcare, Portugal also offers a range of private health insurance options. Private healthcare in Portugal is known for its high standards of care and shorter waiting times for appointments and procedures. Many expats choose to supplement their public healthcare coverage with private insurance to ensure they have access to a wider range of services and specialists.

Retiring Abroad: Portugal Edition for Adults Looking for a New Beginning

When seeking medical care in Portugal, it is important to have a basic understanding of the healthcare system and how to navigate it as an expat. This includes registering for a user card, choosing a primary care physician, and understanding the process for accessing specialist care or emergency services. By familiarizing yourself with the healthcare system early on, you can ensure a smooth transition and access the care you need when you need it.

Overall, accessing medical care as an expat in Portugal is a straightforward process that offers high-quality, affordable healthcare options. Whether you choose to utilize the public healthcare system or opt for private insurance, you can rest assured knowing that you will have access to the medical care you need to enjoy a healthy and fulfilling retirement in this beautiful country.

Retiring Abroad: Portugal Edition for Adults Looking for a New Beginning

Retiring Abroad: Portugal Edition for Adults Looking for a New Beginning

Chapter 5: Adjusting to Life in Portugal

Learning the Language and Culture

Learning the language and culture of your new home country is an essential step in successfully retiring abroad in Portugal. While many Portuguese people speak English, making an effort to learn the language will not only help you navigate daily tasks but also show respect for the local culture. Consider enrolling in language classes or using language learning apps to improve your Portuguese skills.

Understanding the culture of Portugal is equally important as mastering the language. From the traditional Fado music to the delicious cuisine, immersing yourself in the local customs and traditions will enhance your retirement experience. Take the time to explore the local markets, attend cultural events, and interact with the friendly locals to fully embrace the Portuguese way of life.

Retiring Abroad: Portugal Edition for Adults Looking for a New Beginning

One of the best ways to learn the language and culture of Portugal is by forming connections with the local community. Joining expat groups or social clubs can provide you with opportunities to practice your Portuguese, make new friends, and participate in cultural activities. Building relationships with locals can also help you feel more integrated into your new surroundings and create a sense of belonging in your retirement.

As you continue to learn the language and culture of Portugal, be patient with yourself and embrace the process of cultural adaptation. It may take time to feel comfortable speaking Portuguese and understanding the nuances of the local customs, but with perseverance and an open mind, you will gradually become more fluent and culturally aware. Remember that retirement abroad is a journey of personal growth and discovery, and learning the language and culture of Portugal is an enriching part of that experience.

In conclusion, investing time and effort into learning the language and culture of Portugal is a valuable endeavor for adults looking to retire in this beautiful country. By immersing yourself in the local language, customs, and traditions, you will not only enhance your retirement experience but also forge deeper connections with the Portuguese people. Embrace the opportunity to expand your horizons and embrace a new way of life in Portugal as you embark on this exciting chapter of retirement abroad.

Making Friends and Building a Social Network

Making friends and building a social network is crucial when retiring abroad, especially in a new and unfamiliar country like Portugal. As adults looking for a new beginning in this beautiful country, it is important to establish connections and create a sense of community to make your retirement experience more fulfilling and enjoyable.

Retiring Abroad: Portugal Edition for Adults Looking for a New Beginning

One of the best ways to make friends in Portugal is to get involved in local activities and social events. Whether it's joining a local club or organization, attending cultural festivals, or taking part in community classes, putting yourself out there and engaging with others is a great way to meet like-minded individuals and build your social network.

Another way to make friends in Portugal is to reach out to expat communities and online forums. These platforms provide a great opportunity to connect with other retirees who are also looking to build a social network and share experiences. Online platforms can also be a helpful resource for finding local events and activities where you can meet new people.

Building a social network in Portugal also involves being open to new experiences and stepping out of your comfort zone. Whether it's striking up a conversation with a neighbor, attending a language exchange meetup, or simply exploring the local neighborhood, being proactive and friendly can go a long way in making new connections and friendships.

Retiring Abroad: Portugal Edition for Adults Looking for a New Beginning

Overall, making friends and building a social network in Portugal is essential for a successful retirement experience. By actively seeking out opportunities to meet new people, engaging in local activities, and being open to new experiences, you can create a supportive community of friends and acquaintances who will enrich your life in this new chapter of retirement abroad.

Exploring Leisure Activities and Hobbies in Portugal

As you settle into your new life in Portugal, it's important to find activities and hobbies that bring you joy and fulfillment. Luckily, Portugal offers a wide range of leisure activities that cater to all interests and preferences. Whether you enjoy exploring the great outdoors, immersing yourself in the local culture, or simply relaxing with a good book, there is something for everyone in this vibrant and diverse country.

Retiring Abroad: Portugal Edition for Adults Looking for a New Beginning

One of the most popular leisure activities in Portugal is hiking. With its stunning landscapes, from rugged coastlines to lush green forests, Portugal is a hiker's paradise. There are countless trails and paths to explore, ranging from easy strolls to challenging hikes for the more experienced adventurer. Whether you prefer a leisurely walk along the beach or a steep climb up a mountain, you'll find plenty of opportunities to get out and enjoy the fresh air and beautiful scenery.

For those who prefer a more relaxed pace, Portugal also offers a wealth of cultural activities to enjoy. From visiting historic sites and museums to attending traditional festivals and concerts, there is always something happening in Portugal to keep you entertained. Whether you're interested in history, art, music, or cuisine, you'll find plenty of opportunities to immerse yourself in the rich cultural heritage of this fascinating country.

Retiring Abroad: Portugal Edition for Adults Looking for a New Beginning

If you're looking for a more hands-on hobby, why not try your hand at traditional Portuguese crafts? From pottery and weaving to tile painting and cork carving, there are endless opportunities to learn new skills and create beautiful works of art. Many local artisans offer classes and workshops for beginners, so you can start exploring your creative side and connect with the local community through your shared love of craftsmanship.

No matter what your interests or hobbies may be, Portugal has something to offer you. Whether you're looking to stay active, learn something new, or simply relax and unwind, you'll find plenty of opportunities to enjoy yourself in this welcoming and vibrant country. So go ahead, explore all that Portugal has to offer and make the most of your retirement in this beautiful corner of the world.

Chapter 6: Legal and Financial Considerations for Expats in Portugal

Understanding Tax Obligations as an Expat in Portugal

As an expat living in Portugal, it's important to understand your tax obligations in order to ensure compliance with local laws and regulations. Portugal has a unique tax system that may differ from what you are used to in your home country. By familiarizing yourself with the tax laws in Portugal, you can avoid any potential issues or penalties.

One of the first things to be aware of as an expat in Portugal is the residency rules that determine your tax status. In general, if you are a resident in Portugal for more than 183 days in a calendar year, you are considered a tax resident and are subject to Portuguese tax laws. This means that you will need to report your worldwide income to the Portuguese tax authorities.

Retiring Abroad: Portugal Edition for Adults Looking for a New Beginning

Portugal has a progressive tax system, with tax rates ranging from 14.5% to 48%. Income from employment, pensions, rental income, and capital gains are all subject to taxation in Portugal. It's important to keep detailed records of your income and expenses in order to accurately report your tax liability to the authorities.

As an expat in Portugal, you may also be eligible for certain tax benefits or exemptions. For example, Portugal offers a special tax regime for non-habitual residents, which can provide significant tax savings for retirees and other expats. It's important to consult with a tax professional or financial advisor to see if you qualify for any of these benefits.

By understanding your tax obligations as an expat in Portugal, you can ensure that you are in compliance with local laws and regulations. Being proactive about your tax responsibilities can help you avoid any potential issues or penalties down the road. Take the time to educate yourself on the tax laws in Portugal and seek professional advice if needed to make the most of your expat experience in this beautiful country.

Estate Planning and Inheritance Laws in Portugal

Estate planning and inheritance laws in Portugal are essential topics for anyone considering retiring in this beautiful country. Understanding how these laws work can help you ensure that your assets are distributed according to your wishes after your passing. In Portugal, inheritance laws are based on the principle of forced heirship, which means that a portion of your estate must be left to your legal heirs, such as children or spouses.

When it comes to estate planning in Portugal, it is important to consult with a local lawyer who is familiar with the intricacies of the country's legal system. This is especially true if you have assets in multiple countries or complex family situations. A lawyer can help you draft a will that reflects your wishes and complies with Portuguese law. They can also advise you on the best way to structure your assets to minimize taxes and ensure a smooth transfer of wealth to your heirs.

Retiring Abroad: Portugal Edition for Adults Looking for a New Beginning

One important aspect of estate planning in Portugal is the process of probate, which is the legal procedure for validating a will and distributing the deceased's assets. Probate can be a lengthy and complex process, so it is important to plan ahead and make sure your affairs are in order. By working with a lawyer and setting up a comprehensive estate plan, you can help your loved ones avoid unnecessary stress and confusion during a difficult time.

In Portugal, inheritance tax is levied on the value of the assets inherited by each beneficiary. The tax rates vary depending on the relationship between the deceased and the beneficiary, with spouses and children generally receiving more favorable treatment. By understanding the tax implications of your estate plan, you can make informed decisions that maximize the value of your assets for your heirs.

Overall, estate planning and inheritance laws in Portugal are important considerations for anyone looking to retire in this charming country. By working with a local lawyer and taking the time to understand the legal framework, you can ensure that your assets are protected and your wishes are respected. With careful planning and the right guidance, you can enjoy peace of mind knowing that your loved ones will be taken care of after you are gone.

Setting Up Bank Accounts and Managing Finances in Portugal

Setting up bank accounts and managing finances in Portugal is an essential step for anyone looking to retire in this beautiful country. As an adult considering a new beginning in Portugal, it's important to understand the local banking system and how to make the most of your financial resources. By following these tips and guidelines, you can ensure that your retirement in Portugal is as comfortable and stress-free as possible.

Retiring Abroad: Portugal Edition for Adults Looking for a New Beginning

When setting up a bank account in Portugal, it's crucial to choose a reputable financial institution with a strong presence in the country. Look for banks that offer English-speaking services and have a range of products tailored to expats and retirees. It's also important to consider factors like fees, interest rates, and online banking options when selecting a bank. Take the time to research different banks and compare their offerings before making a decision.

Once you have opened a bank account in Portugal, it's important to manage your finances effectively to make the most of your retirement savings. Create a budget that outlines your monthly expenses and income, and stick to it to avoid overspending. Consider setting up automatic transfers to your savings account to ensure that you are saving for the future. Keep track of your transactions and regularly review your financial statements to stay on top of your finances.

Retiring Abroad: Portugal Edition for Adults Looking for a New Beginning

When managing your finances in Portugal, it's also important to be aware of any tax implications that may affect your retirement income. Consult with a financial advisor or tax professional to understand your tax obligations as an expat retiree in Portugal. This will help you avoid any surprises and ensure that you are compliant with local tax laws. By staying informed and proactive about your finances, you can enjoy a worry-free retirement in Portugal.

In conclusion, setting up bank accounts and managing finances in Portugal is a crucial aspect of retiring in this beautiful country. By choosing the right bank, creating a budget, and staying informed about tax obligations, you can ensure that your retirement in Portugal is financially secure. With careful planning and smart financial management, you can make the most of your retirement savings and enjoy a comfortable and fulfilling life in Portugal.

Chapter 7: Conclusion

Reflecting on Your Decision to Retire in Portugal

As you sit back and reflect on your decision to retire in Portugal, you may find yourself filled with a mix of emotions - excitement, anticipation, and perhaps a hint of nervousness. It's perfectly normal to feel a range of emotions when making such a significant life change. Remember, you've made the decision to embark on a new chapter in your life, one that offers endless possibilities and opportunities for growth.

When considering retiring in Portugal, it's important to take the time to reflect on what drew you to this beautiful country in the first place. Was it the stunning landscapes, the rich history and culture, or the warm and welcoming people? Whatever it may be, remind yourself of the reasons why Portugal stood out to you as the perfect place to spend your retirement years.

Retiring Abroad: Portugal Edition for Adults Looking for a New Beginning

As you reflect on your decision, think about the lifestyle you envision for yourself in Portugal. Do you see yourself strolling through cobblestone streets, enjoying a leisurely meal at a local cafe, or simply taking in the breathtaking views of the Atlantic Ocean? Consider how these experiences align with your values and priorities, and how they contribute to your overall sense of happiness and fulfillment.

It's also important to reflect on the practical aspects of retiring in Portugal. Consider factors such as healthcare, cost of living, and ease of access to amenities and services. Take the time to research and plan accordingly, so that you can make the most of your retirement years in this vibrant and welcoming country.

In the end, reflecting on your decision to retire in Portugal is an opportunity to reaffirm your commitment to this new chapter in your life. Embrace the excitement and embrace the challenges that come with starting fresh in a new country. Remember, you have chosen Portugal for a reason, and the experiences and memories that await you are sure to make this decision one of the best you've ever made.

Retiring Abroad: Portugal Edition for Adults Looking for a New Beginning

Tips for a Smooth Transition to Expat Life in Portugal

Moving to a new country can be both exciting and overwhelming, especially when it comes to retiring abroad. Portugal is a popular destination for retirees looking for a new beginning, with its beautiful landscapes, rich culture, and welcoming communities. To ensure a smooth transition to expat life in Portugal, here are some tips to help you make the most of your new adventure.

First and foremost, it's important to familiarize yourself with the local customs and traditions of Portugal. Take the time to learn about the country's history, cuisine, and language. This will not only help you to feel more at home in your new surroundings but will also show respect for the local culture.

Another important tip for a smooth transition to expat life in Portugal is to connect with other expats and local residents. Join expat groups or social clubs in your area to meet new people and make friends. This will help you to build a support network and feel more connected to your new community.

Retiring Abroad: Portugal Edition for Adults Looking for a New Beginning

When it comes to practical matters, such as healthcare and finances, it's essential to do your research and plan ahead. Make sure you understand the healthcare system in Portugal and have the necessary insurance coverage. Additionally, consult with a financial advisor to ensure that your retirement savings and investments are in order for your move abroad.

One of the best ways to immerse yourself in Portuguese culture is to explore the country's many attractions and events. Visit historic sites, attend local festivals, and sample traditional cuisine to fully experience all that Portugal has to offer. By embracing the local lifestyle, you'll not only enrich your retirement experience but also create lasting memories.

In conclusion, transitioning to expat life in Portugal can be a rewarding and fulfilling experience for retirees looking for a new beginning. By following these tips and approaching your move with an open mind and positive attitude, you'll be well on your way to creating a happy and fulfilling life in your new home. Enjoy the journey!

Resources for Expats Living in Portugal

If you're considering retiring in Portugal, there are plenty of resources available to help make your transition as smooth as possible. From legal and financial advice to social clubs and expat communities, Portugal offers a wealth of resources for expats looking to make the most of their retirement years in this beautiful country.

One of the first things you'll want to do when moving to Portugal is to familiarize yourself with the country's legal and financial systems. Whether you need help navigating the residency process, setting up a bank account, or understanding the tax implications of retiring abroad, there are plenty of professionals and organizations available to assist you. Consider reaching out to a local lawyer or financial advisor who specializes in expat issues to ensure you have all the information you need to make informed decisions.

Retiring Abroad: Portugal Edition for Adults Looking for a New Beginning

In addition to legal and financial resources, there are also a variety of social clubs and expat communities in Portugal that can help you connect with like-minded individuals and build a support network in your new home. Whether you're interested in playing golf, learning Portuguese, or simply socializing with other expats, there are plenty of opportunities to get involved and make new friends. Consider joining a local expat group or attending community events to start building connections and feeling at home in Portugal.

For those looking for more specialized assistance, there are also relocation services available in Portugal that can help with everything from finding a place to live to setting up utilities and getting connected with healthcare providers. These services can be particularly helpful for older adults who may need extra support during the moving process. Consider reaching out to a relocation specialist to discuss your needs and see how they can help make your transition to Portugal as smooth as possible.

Retiring Abroad: Portugal Edition for Adults Looking for a New Beginning

Overall, Portugal offers a wealth of resources for expats looking to retire in this beautiful country. Whether you need legal and financial advice, social connections, or specialized assistance with your move, there are plenty of professionals and organizations available to help. By taking advantage of these resources, you can make the most of your retirement years in Portugal and enjoy all that this vibrant country has to offer.

Retiring Abroad: Portugal Edition for Adults Looking for a New Beginning

Retiring Abroad: Portugal Edition for Adults Looking for a New Beginning

Retiring Abroad: Portugal Edition for Adults Looking for a New Beginning

Retiring In Portugal Yes Please!

www.ingramcontent.com/pod-product-compliance
Lightning Source LLC
Chambersburg PA
CBHW050242230526
45470CB00005B/2080